Contents

1. How to be Happy – An Overview 6
2. The ABCs of Happiness 8
3. The Secret of Happiness 10
4. Where to Begin Your Quest for Happiness 11
   - Possible Locations for Happiness 11
   - Where to start your Quest 11
5. Characteristics of a Psychologically Healthy, Happy Person ... 13
   - Specific and Evident Characteristics of Self-Actualizing People 13
6. Is Happiness a Conscious Ultimate Concern? 15
   - Your Goal fixes your happiness level 15
   - Is it possible to make Happiness your Conscious and Ultimate Concern? 15
7. Why is it Wrong to Make Happiness Your Top Goal? 17
8. How to Focus Your Energy and Intelligence to Attain Happiness 19
9. How Satisfaction of Values Determine Our Happiness 21
10. Learn How to Be Happy – Preparing Your Self-Development Plan 23
11. How to Control Your Emotions 25
    - Factors helpful in controlling your Emotions 25
12. The External and Internal Routes to Happiness 27
13. Using Self-Exploration and Problem-Solving Skills to Achieve Happiness 29
14. Six Steps to Find the Underlying, Internal Causes of Unhappiness 31
15. How to Make Radical or Lifestyle Changes to Attain Greater Happiness 33

16. How to Know What Will Make You Happy 35
17. How to Resolve Your Conflicts to Bring Happiness................. 37
18. Self-Actualization – Learn to Attain Higher Self Power............ 39
19. How to Imagine and Create an Internal Model of Happiness in Your Mind.. 41
20. Two Worldviews - Negative versus Positive Thinking 43
21. How Can You Be Happy in an Imperfect World? 45
    How to be happy amid such imperfections 45
22. Deficit Motivation vs. Abundance Motivation 47
23. How to Develop Positive Thinking and Feel Happier in Everyday Life 49
24. Increasing Your Self-Worth to Get Greater Happiness 51
25. How to Develop a Positive Self-Image....................................... 53
26. Learn to Accept Self and Others 55
27. How to Be More Self-Confident... 57
28. Using External vs. Internal Expectations to Evaluate Yourself 59
29. Sources of Dependency and External Control 61
30. Sources of Internal Control 63
31. How to Be Internally Directed and Effective with Others......... 65
32. How to Control Other People 67
33. How to Achieve Peak Functioning of Your Mind and Body..... 69
34. Optimal Learning as the Basis of Happiness............................ 71
35. How Does Harmonious Functioning Affect Happiness............ 73
36. How Does Harmonious Functioning Affect Emotions 75
37. How Mental Control Increases Your Level of Happiness......... 77
38. Learn to Be a Master of Your Emotions 79
39. Resolve Your Inner Conflicts to Bring Harmony and Happiness 81
40. Looking at a Problem from a Higher Level of Understanding. 83
41. How to Overcome Depression and other Negative Emotions. 85

42. How to Overcome Grief, Sadness and Apathy in Your Life 87

43. How to Lower Your Anxiety and Stress and Increase Confidence 89

44. Learn to Be Happy in All Situations 91

45. How to Funnel Your Energy to Maximize Happiness 93

46. How to Stay in Control of Your Life and Be Happy 95

47. How to Achieve Your Goals in Life and Be Happy 97

48. How to Manage Your Time and Create Happiness in Your Life 99

49. Your Checklist about How to Be Happy 101

1. How to be Happy – An Overview

Happiness is an emotion and, ideally, an individualistic view. To you, happiness is something different from what somebody else feels. It is a particular state of mind. Everybody has different views on happiness and so, the ways of attaining happiness will differ from person to person.

Normally, happiness is synonymous with joy, well-being, delight, love, safety, and health.

The term, "happiness' traces its origins to the Greek 'Eudaimonia', which means being a good soul. It refers to having virtuous habits through moral and honorable deeds. However, people define happiness differently. It is a culmination of achievement of specific ideals like (not in particular order) health, family, money, physical appearance, intelligence and humor.

It can be spiritual and refer to attaining certain goals. Every culture has their own idea of what makes them happy. And, every person in that same culture will find happiness in different levels. To some, happiness can be praying that there will be supper and supper appears. Happiness means different things to different people.

You can take for an example, a person with an attractive appearance with clothes of the latest fashion and that person will feel happiness. Now, take a lack of either attractiveness or the latest design clothes and a person can have lower self-esteem, which could hurt their feeling of happiness.

Another group defines happiness as a fulfilling life according to one's ideals. Normally, you can attain such happiness through dedication, hard work, and sacrifice.

It is not possible to define happiness in definitive terms, as it is a subjective feeling. It is an internal experience and characterizing or labeling it in clear language terms may be a difficult, if not an impossible, proposition.

Happiness is often associated with feeling content. Satisfaction is the key to achievement. You find contentment in trusted family, friends, or community relationships. You have to open your feelings, talk, and discuss things to experience happiness. Again, happiness comes by talking about topics of your interest. A music lover may not find sports interesting and may not find happiness in such discussions.

Engaging and immersing yourself in what you excel at is a source of happiness. Such engagement leads to contentment, producing happiness. Looking forward to something like a vacation brings happiness. An optimistic focus of life, with the view that the glass is half-full, creates feelings of happiness.

Happiness is the utmost in giving unto others. Happiness is within you and you can experience it by sharing with others.

Happiness can be momentary, such as setting a goal and reaching it. The feeling of euphoria that one can get with reaching a goal can be happiness.

Let's see what you can do to become a happier person.

2. The ABCs of Happiness

Happiness is a subjective feeling. So, you determine happiness by your preconceived views and opinions of what should happen or not, by the incidence of an event. You are guided by your thinking, rather than occurrence of the event.

This is the main determinant of people locating and identifying happy situations everywhere.

In simple language, you should accept events as they happen without giving any credence to pros and cons of the event, its occurrence, implications on future events and so on. Your ideas about happiness or occurrence of events governing your happiness levels fall within certain segments. These segments define your philosophy and beliefs on life.

Such a clear proposition does not engulf you in different negative emotions like fear, anger, and depression or shame. They, therefore, do not preclude the presence of your greatest positive emotion - happiness.

You should proceed by stressing on the 'It could be better' factor rather than 'It should' factor. The first proposition highlights your compromising and rational attitude, while the second tends directly to anger, a negative feeling pulling you away from happiness.

Feelings of shame can arise if you are unable to perform or reach accepted achievement levels in society. This could be about anything like your smartness, reputation, family background, and similar facts.

Shame is self-disapproval or criticism for not being able to attain accepted norms. Accept such incidents as occurrences in life and look ahead to overcome obstacles on your way to achieving happiness.

Dwelling on past mistakes is not the road to happiness. You must learn to forgive yourself for mistakes and learn from them as a lesson in life. Punishing yourself over and over for mistakes is painful and will hinder future attempts at finding happiness.

Depression arises from irrational thinking. It is also a culmination of all negative emotions, leading to lack of self-confidence. The underlying cure for depression lies within you. You have to love yourself first to be able to love and receive love from all. This opens doors to your happiness and success.

Fear is worry about your ability. You should be brave enough to allay your fears and confront them. Do not lie low and accept everything. Instead, strive to do beyond your expectations. This focus is more likely to bring you happiness.

3. The Secret of Happiness

The secret of happiness lies in your decision to be happy.

Happiness is missing in you if you fill your mind and heart with weary and dreary thoughts. You disturb your state of mind with doubts and set preconditions for attaining a level of happiness.

If you are able to meet your conditions, you are happy. If not, you may be unhappy and depressed. Hence, you decide about functioning of your brain and set preconditions for your feelings of joy or happiness. However, the irony is that once you meet the said conditions, you decide on another set of conditions. This goes on and so, happiness evades you or, rather, you do not allow happiness to come near you.

The secret of happiness lies in your continuous decision to remain happy, whatever be the circumstances. You should enjoy your journey to reach your set goals.

Some people tend to stress over the activities and behavior of other people as determinants of their happiness. Your happiness is yours and you must not blame others for the lack of your happiness. You control your mind, your thoughts, and hence, you hold the sole decision toward your own happiness.

Simple solutions to secure happiness are to be optimistic and look to the present without worrying about the future or the past. Boost your confidence levels to attain higher self-esteem by being true to self, and always striving forward.

4. Where to Begin Your Quest for Happiness

Happiness does not only mean feeling joy; it can be a feeling of peace, serenity, and tranquility. Rather, happiness is something, which pushes away all negative emotions like stress, sadness, anger, guilt, depression, and apathy. All these stressful emotions are often the cause of many illnesses like cancer, cardiovascular diseases, AIDS, and other infections.

Possible Locations for Happiness

You could look for happiness at different locations like your family, friends, career, and education. Your aim is to do away with negative occurrences like illness, poverty, failure, rejection and other difficult situations. Hence, your key to happiness lies in striving and rising above such negativities to attain the level of happiness.

Where to start your Quest

The foundation of your happiness lies in your choice to be happy. You have to commit yourself to be happy and make it the most important aim of your life. The onus of your happiness is with you and you cannot transfer this responsibility to anybody else. You also cannot hold anybody else responsible for causing you unhappiness. Both happiness and unhappiness lies within you and you alone can make the right choice of the two.

Although there are different social organizations, self-help books, and counselors to help you in your quest for happiness, nothing works better than your own effort for your quest for happiness. The first step towards this quest lies in prioritizing your personal growth.

Set goals, achieve, and then set higher achievement levels for yourself. Do not overdo your goals as then it could lead to more unhappiness if you keep setting goals one after another. Focus on realistic and practical goals.

Consider an obstacle as an opportunity to grow and reach closer to your goals. Your failures are your steps to your success. Do not brood over your disappointments and look beyond them. Learn from your mistakes and proceed towards your main goal of being happy.

Become mentally strong to deal with all hurdles and become capable of dealing with difficult situations. Locate role models like happy and successful people to start with your quest for happiness. Look deep into their attempts to overcome depression, stress, and other negative emotions and come out as a highly successful person in life.

5. Characteristics of a Psychologically Healthy, Happy Person

A psychologically happy and healthy person achieves happiness and strives to go beyond through process of self-actualization. Dr. Abraham Maslow, father of humanistic psychology, has shed light on various characteristics prevalent in a healthy and psychologically happy person. Of course, Dr. Maslow was himself a self-actualizing person. Most such happy persons are the key contributors to the health and happiness of the society and community as a whole.

Specific and Evident Characteristics of Self-Actualizing People

A happy and healthy person dispels following individualistic uniqueness in his personality and character:

Stoic acceptance of the facts of life without questioning their occurrence

Humanity encompasses not only family and friends but also everyone and everything interacting with human existence

Perceiving, believing, and reasoning truth and dwelling deeper in to the surreal realities to develop accurate perceptions in life

Such perceptions help understand and mark clear discriminations between right and wrong or good and evil

Resolving conflicts easily because of their easy acceptance of the basic philosophies of life

An aura of calm and peace with themselves and therefore able to focus on higher realms of life and consequent happiness

Avoiding being self-centered and being more creative due to intense naivety and spontaneity

Placing greater importance on the character and values of a person rather than materialistic parameters and concentrating on problem solving rather than on its occurrence.

Simple, spontaneous, and natural existence placing high value on essential habits and emphasizing higher-level values like Meta values

Dr. Maslow stressed that you need to meet and satisfy lower and basic needs like safety, health, belonging, love, and status before proceeding to higher Meta values. Such higher Meta values include simplicity, perfection, completion, goodness, uniqueness, honesty, justified approach, and a feeling of continuing aliveness invigorating everything.

Psychologically healthy and happy people support a free mind and proceed towards a more productive and peaceful phase. However, if there arises any danger to their basic values in life, they still proceed ahead toward their higher goals without perceiving any danger to their basic values. The broader perspective of such happy people differentiates them from the other commoners.

6. Is Happiness a Conscious Ultimate Concern?

Your ultimate concern in life determines your goal in life. The same is true if you say it the other way round. Your goal in life determines the ultimate concern in life. Hence, you have to analyze your inner self to arrive at what is your topmost concern in life. You obviously work concentrating towards attainment of this sole aim or goal in life.

Your Goal fixes your happiness level

Following from that, your aim or ultimate concern determines your happiness level. Hence, you are making a conscious effort towards attainment of happiness by arriving at your main goal in life. Paul Tillich, theologian and philosopher of the modern era, stresses that your entire existence, personality, and life itself depends on attainment of happiness through satisfaction of your goals.

Different individuals place importance on different ideals in life like money, love, happiness, family values, education, and the list goes on. The underlying functioning of your instincts finds governance through such ideals. If at any time something comes in your way towards attainment of your main goal, your main aim will be the eternal winner of this conflict.

Is it possible to make Happiness your Conscious and Ultimate Concern?

Sure, why not?

Often people decide from many goals like money, social status, or career status their main goal in life. They feel that fulfillment of these goals can bring them happiness. It sure can. Nevertheless, if you place maximum stress on attainment of these goals alone as your end happiness, then any disturbances in attaining or if you are unable to attain set goals, you become unhappy.

You lose your level of happiness. You remain so very much focused on attaining set goals that you forego many happy experiences on your path to happiness. Hence, you trade happiness for your goal in life. Ultimately, non-attainment of desired levels of goals in life only contributes to your unhappiness.

Therefore, making happiness your ultimate concern is a better proposition. Here you evaluate every activity as to which yields you more happiness. Therefore, you only trade happiness for more happiness.

7. Why is it Wrong to Make Happiness Your Top Goal?

Making happiness your goal in life is a subjective fact. Yet, many are reluctant to disclose that happiness is their ultimate concern in life. In that case, you need to understand the route to your happiness or the means you adopt to achieve happiness and satisfy your most important goal in life.

Immanuel Kant poses a maxim for attainment of happiness. Kant stresses that the end universal aim of all rational beings is attainment of happiness. The underlying fear of making happiness the sole aim in your life stems from the probability of turning selfish and centered on achieving happiness through any means. Here you need to distinguish between your means of attaining happiness.

Happiness and success go hand in hand. If you are ready to sacrifice your happiness for the sake or success of others, then you cannot be happy, as the other person would also try to sacrifice his happiness for yours. Ultimately, no one is happy.

There is a subtle but clear line of demarcation between pleasure and happiness. Lower brain centers function to meet the needs of these centers like hunger, touch, thirst, and others. However, making pleasure the main goal in life makes you addicted to such thrills. It does not yield happiness. Pleasure also assumes the character of selfishness and at times, transforms you into a criminal. This is because pleasure is irrespective of any care for other's needs or feelings.

However, happiness is on an entirely different strata. The highest brain centers function towards attainment of higher values in life like truth, love, beauty, and similar others. This deviates from the normal pleasure-seeking attitude and hence, is away from selfishness.

Therefore, giving brings greater happiness than selfishness. Self-interest at a higher level provides a balanced parameter of giving to others or giving to self. Here, therefore, making happiness your prime goal in life does not pose any problems. Hence, you are not wrong in making happiness your top goal.

Similarly, conscious effort in making happiness your goal is not necessary. Instead, achievement of other associated goals could lead to happiness. Rather, happiness is an accepted and welcomed by-product of this occurrence.

8. How to Focus Your Energy and Intelligence to Attain Happiness

Your aim in life could be to attain happiness. You can attain happiness through various means, which are in a way your goals too. Such goals could be feeling of love, personal success, success in career, or intelligence. Again, all such adjectives have a definition of their own. Your perception of success may not be the same as that of the society. Hence, your satisfaction at your success cannot be on the same level in society.

In all, success and its measure is a subjective tool. Therefore, you have to analyze your perception of success and decide on its degree. You have to fix your priority levels and seek answer to the question - What is most important to you?

Accordingly, if your answer is happiness other aims like career success, personal success, love, or anything else is only a means to attain your ultimate goal of happiness. Therefore, you can measure your happiness by your levels in these subsidiary goals.

Similarly, your ability to transform these paths of happiness positively is an important point for seeking happiness. You have to focus your intelligence and energy towards fulfillment of these goals. Dr. Wayne Dyer dwells on a similar concept in his book- 'Happiness IQ?' Your capacity to perceive and arrive at the solutions to your problems is your intelligence. Therefore, intelligence produces positive results for happiness.

Similarly, happiness needs to be giving unto others for being with you or for you to be happy. You cannot be happy by causing unhappiness to others. Stressing on your means to happiness alone is good no doubt. At the same time, this stress should not be at the cost of unhappiness of others or without giving any credence to basic values in life.

In that case, you become a mere machine pursuing your goal and you cannot locate happiness anywhere. Rather, you have lost your way to happiness in your attempt to acquire something materialistic. Therefore, keep your means of attaining happiness alive and do not allow it to die in your milieu to attain happiness.

9. How Satisfaction of Values Determine Our Happiness

You assign certain values as your measuring stones to happiness.

These inner values could be the ones to satisfy your biological needs and yield happiness. It could also be the Meta values belonging to the upper category of values like truth, spirituality, and sublime beauty bringing in happiness. Hence, your satisfaction of values is a major determinant of your happiness.

You can evaluate your level of happiness by listing your categories of happiness like career, family, friends, and health, financial stability, and so on. Rate your happiness in each category on the same scale and construct a happiness graph with these values. A yearly progress of the graph determines your level of happiness.

Your different parameters of success depend on your perspectives of each parameter. If you feel you can be happier by succeeding in your career, you contribute to a happiness level in one area only. Each of your perspectives is a pillar for the foundation of your goal of happiness.

Hence, success in each sphere contributes equally to your happiness. This also extends to your lending happiness to others. In the same vein, you can say that you are able to make others happy and be happy yourself too.

Every perspective needs coordination. If you are confused about any of your perceptions to success and consequent happiness, clear it at the onset. Proceeding with a confused mind is to progress without any clear conceptions, rather a blind approach. This just cannot lead you anywhere. Therefore, your happiness remains elusive.

Clear your confusion as it often leads to monotony. A confused state of affairs cannot locate anything conclusive anywhere. Therefore, it is equal to staring into a blank space. This is the onset of boredom. Your efforts at securing happiness can bog you down.

You can rekindle your efforts by seeking newer avenues and developing better patterns for attaining happiness. You therefore, have to assess your capabilities, strengths, weaknesses, beliefs, and other guidelines to progress on your path to happiness. Satisfying each of these parameters alone can determine your level of happiness.

10. Learn How to Be Happy – Preparing Your Self-Development Plan

You can draft a self-development plan to achieve happiness by following these steps:

Although happiness is your prime goal, you need to place equal stress on truth, health, love, and similar others as your means to attain happiness. Neglecting or placing excessive importance on any one goal disturbs your formation for attaining happiness.

Probe deeper into your self to diagnose and eliminate causes for your unhappiness. Instead, stimulate your happiness producing elements.

Develop feelings of higher category like spirituality, love, and truth with a positive attitude towards life.

Conquer your fears and cultivate confidence and accompanying peace within your inner self. Although you should hope for the best, being prepared for the worst is the best way to build up your inner strength.

Accept yourself and others unconditionally. Overcome your negativity to create space for the positive feelings to settle. Improve on all your capabilities to develop an overall complete and fulfilled image.

Be self-dependent, confident and avoid overt need of others. Maintain assertiveness and develop a controlled relationship with all.

Rise above the negativities of life like anger, frustration, anxiety, fear, jealousy, resentment, and similar others. Aim for a harmonious functioning of your total self.

Continue learning and developing newer patterns of achieving success and consequent happiness. Do not become static and try to be happy in all situations.

11. How to Control Your Emotions

Emotions reflect your inner state at any particular moment. If you are angry or unhappy about something, you find expression through your words or your mood displays your emotions. Similarly, if you are ecstatic or overly happy about something, your exuberance displays your innermost feeling of happiness. Therefore, your outer self or your face is the mirror of your emotions.

In all, you hold the key to control your emotions. You can choose to become angry or happy over a situation. It could be to your liking or not. However, controlling your emotions changes the face of the situation and your mirror like face depicts your inner self.

Factors helpful in controlling your Emotions

You need to have a commitment towards your inner self to remain happy in any situation. Rather, you have to try to locate sources of happiness even in your dreariest and anguishing moments. If you start developing negative feelings, dissuade them and instead, concentrate on identifying anything positive. This makes not only you a happy person, it also bring happiness to others.

Emotions are a reflection of your inner mind. Therefore, your inner-self decides the outcome of any event. The event is no doubt an external occurrence but your perception of that event comes from within you. Hence, your thoughts and feelings govern your emotions.

To control your emotions, you need to control your feelings. You can do this by instilling positive thoughts, creating a positive atmosphere around you, and overcoming negativities everywhere. You cannot disown or refuse to accept the presence of negativity. It is only your self-power to overcome negativity and recognize the presence and effects of optimism.

Your speech displays your inner emotions. Hence, modulate your speech to express confidence in large measures. Avoid excuses, as they are a direct reflection of your stress and inabilities. It also shows your helplessness in a situation.

Convert your beliefs in to your speech pattern and use them to deal with any eventualities. A self-confident person can take over all obstacles and progress on the path to achieving happiness for yourself and others.

12. The External and Internal Routes to Happiness

Every person wants to be happy in life. However, happiness is something that may prove to be difficult to attain. A person may be highly successful, yet he or she may be living with deep sadness.

Though happiness eludes many of us, there are things that we can do to achieve it. Some routes to happiness are external, while some are internal. The external routes may include any action or association in relation to our external environment. Our external activities like eating, sleeping, talking, playing, working, etc. have their bearing on our inner being. When we are feeling low, some of these activities may prove to be effective in lifting our spirits. For instance, taking up a new hobby such as playing golf or joining a music band or just learning to cook some new dish may have magical effect on your state of mind.

In our external activities, we can set different kinds of goals to ourselves and pursue those with passion. These goals may include earning money, making friends, getting a particular job or attaining a goal or a material possession. We attain happiness when we set some goal and achieve it through our efforts.

With the external elements, our inner being also plays an important role in deciding whether we are happy or not. The internal route to happiness revolves around our entire thought process and mental makeup. A person needs to have a strong internal world to remain happy, because we are what we think we are.

To be happy, it is important to develop a higher self-esteem. It allows one to love self and others. Another important requirement is to develop a positive worldview. Rather than being upset over the things that we have not attained, we should learn to appreciate the things that we have gained. Being positive towards life and overcoming the negative thought process is necessary for happiness. You should have good role models and take inspiration from their stories of struggle and triumph.

13. Using Self-Exploration and Problem-Solving Skills to Achieve Happiness

Being happy may prove to be too difficult a task. It may take our greatest efforts to attain happiness. Even though there is no magic formula for happiness, we can try some external and internal routes to happiness. The external routes may vary from taking up a yoga class or making new friends. The internal routes, on the other hand, revolve around our entire thought process and mental makeup. These external and internal routes increase the possibilities of our being happy.

There is hardly an end to problems and challenges. We keep confronting them all the time. We may be feeling mentally down due to health problems, broken relationships or serious losses of money. Even negative thoughts, inner conflicts and other unpleasant events could rob us off our happiness. Happiness lies in exploring and applying our capabilities to tackle these problems and challenges.

However, we need to accept the fact that adding a few positive activities into a very unhappy life could not be the ultimate solution. We can use several "stress reduction techniques" and positive activities to tackle the problems in hand. These could include physical exercise, relaxation training, and visualization techniques. These activities help us effectively deal with our negative emotions.

However, permanent happiness may not come even after taking up these activities. For lasting happiness, it is important to address the root of the problems that we face. These positive activities could supplement our efforts to find actual solutions to our problems.

If a person is depressed due to loss of job, simple relaxation or watching a movie could not be of much use. These activities could provide temporary relief to the person. However, for regaining happiness, the person has to do something to get a job. In such a situation, it is advisable to explore his potential and the existing avenues for finding a better job. Happiness would return once the person gets a job using his or her problem solving skills.

14. Six Steps to Find the Underlying, Internal Causes of Unhappiness

When we feel low, we may feel better using some external routes like playing cards or listening to music. However, for lasting happiness, it is important to find out the underlying, internal causes of happiness.

The following are six steps for finding out these causes:

1. Developing a positive frame of mind

Positive mindset and rational outlook are important for tackling any problem or challenge. Fearing a problem means losing half the battle. Therefore, you should approach the problem with courage. However, you should also be realistic while handling it. You should always be ready to face the truth.

2. Analyzing problem situations

A thorough analysis of a problem situation could help you find out the solution. Have a close look at the sequences and patterns of the events. It will allow you find out how the problem occurred and how best you can handle it.

3. Listening to the inner voice

Emotions are the directing forces for us. They tell us what things are important for us. In a conscious level, we may sometime fail to identify some threats to our expectations, goals, beliefs or inner values. However, some inner part would be aware of such threats and they would direct us through the emotions.

4. Identifying connections with emotions

Many times, we fail to identify different connections with emotions that may lead us to happiness. While some associated thoughts have the potential of bringing us happiness, we remain unmindful to those.

5. Identifying values and beliefs

As you search the roots of your unhappiness, you will start uncovering the underlying issues and subparts, which are responsible for the problems. Identification of these issues and subparts would help you find out a reasonable solution.

6. Setting boundaries of responsibility and control

For solving the emotional issues, it is important to clarify the boundaries of control and responsibility. We need to remember that we cannot control the behavior and action of other people around us. It is our responsibility to control our own behavior in a reasonable way and find happiness. Getting rid of expectations from others would help find the underlying, internal causes of happiness.

Many times you have expectations of others and they fail you.

15. How to Make Radical or Lifestyle Changes to Attain Greater Happiness

A person may need some radical changes in personality and lifestyle to cope with some undesirable circumstances. When the chips are down and things are not going the way we want, some change can help us cope with the situation and attain happiness. However, people usually believe that radical lifestyle changes are either impossible or extremely difficult to make. Even many psychologists believe that way. They believe that it takes some time to assess a person's personality and it takes years to bring radical changes to his or her personality.

However, we keep encountering incidents where people suddenly put a stop to certain behaviors in a radical way. It could leave them happier. For instance, you could see somebody taking drugs for years and one fine day you would find him or her suddenly stopping to take drugs. After quitting drugs, many people lead a normal life leaving the past behind and concentrating on some productive work. You will find many such cases of radical changes in identity, values, goals and their behavior.

People making such radical changes in their lifestyle and behavior pattern usually refer to this whole phenomenon as conversion experience. You would find many people describing their changes as results of achieving some basic insight or finding a new direction in life.

It may not be easy to make some radical changes to attain happiness. However, it is not impossible either. People making such changes usually do it in a very brief period - often in a day. A sudden commitment to change allows them to wipe off their past and start life afresh. However, it is important to consider this commitment to change as the most important value in life. It would enable to move on with the changed behavior pattern. Positive radical lifestyle changes bring us new sets of values, priorities and view of life. All these enable us to work towards the well-being of self and others.

16. How to Know What Will Make You Happy

The road to happiness often proves to be too difficult for many.

The reason we fail to attain happiness is the fact that we fail to identify things that make us happy.

We can consider the reasons of happiness in relation to three different types of mind systems. These are - pleasure and pain (related to lower brain centers), reason and emotion (related to the cognitive system), and empathy and love (related to the Higher Self).

Usually we use pleasure and pain as decision guides in our regular affairs. However, though pleasure indicates fulfillment of the bodily needs, it has certain limitations as a decision guide. Our lower brain centers send out messages about out bodily needs through pleasure and pain. They tell us when we need food, sleep, heat, cold and so on. We need to respond to these messages with appropriate actions to feel pleasure and avoid pain. Even though pleasure makes us content, it can hardly give us long-term happiness. We may buy bodily pleasure using our resources, yet we may remain unhappy.

Reason and emotion are other important elements as decision guides. They relate to our cognitive domain and are above the principle of pleasure and pain. The cognitive system allows us to view our external and internal environments from a broader perspective. We feel happy if our cognitive system finds that we have been able to fulfill our needs. It is important to have harmony within the cognitive system to be happy.

Our higher self is the supreme factor in deciding whether we are happy or not. The higher self is our inner hero that defines the concepts of anxiety and happiness for us. It allows us to have the feelings of empathy and love. The higher self allows us to think and work towards attaining happiness for self and others. To be happy in life, it is important to follow the higher self that often expresses as a positive inner voice. For instance, you may feel a pang while going to do something that is wrong. That pang itself is the inner voice and your higher self.

17. How to Resolve Your Conflicts to Bring Happiness

Your physical body and inner self work in perfect coordination and harmony to conduct your life. Self-actualizing people lead the lives with the greatest satisfaction and contentment. Such people have the most productive and happiest lives. Hence, you need to understand the foundation of their lives to understand the source of their contentment.

Many associate coordinated functioning to be the root cause for a conflict-free existence. Such functioning stems from the self relating to the Higher Self. Religion and associated beliefs help you connect to the Higher Self. You then find the answers to most of your conflicts through such connection with the Higher Self.

Another set of people try to simplify religious beliefs and code them as essential rules of living. They instill such codes for your daily life. Many accept these codes and follow them blindly. You cannot follow specific rules and find harmony in your relationships. Rules are only a means to attain harmony and locate a peaceful end to your conflicts. Following rules as if it is the voice of God is being irrational. You need to believe in the rules and then follow them to resolve your conflicts of mind and heart.

Rules of the highest level insist on giving happiness to self and others. If your religious rules at any time collide with the basic rule of humanity to love all and spread happiness amongst all, then it is not a rule at all. You cannot follow such rules or gain any harmonious end to your conflicts.

Following rules blindly robs your life of any surprises, enjoyment, and enthusiasm. Instead, it gives you depression. This erases all your chances of being happy. Being honest to yourself is an essential element to attain your happiness.

You need to make a conscious decision to be honest about yourself. You should never hide the truth from yourself. Analyze yourself honestly to understand your true self. Your dishonesty creates a conflict within yourself and leads to depression. Hence, you need to choose your belief to be truthful to your inner self and resolve all your conflicts emerging a happier person.

18. Self-Actualization – Learn to Attain Higher Self Power

There are times in our life when we wonder who we really are and we keep searching for the purpose of our life. There are times when you say things that you do not mean, and do things, which you wish you had not done. At times, we feel there are some ideas that lie deep down, in our minds but are left unexpressed. One can be most aware of these areas of our own mind if we talk with ourselves.

Attaining Higher Self means maximum realization of your own self- including your own strengths and weaknesses. As your higher self continues to grow stronger, it will bring you inner peace and contentment. It makes you more confident and a better human being as a whole.

The process involves changing a certain habits. The Higher Self is however, selective about the habits it changes. The habits that are not in tone with the set ideal principles of Higher Self need to be changed, whereas those, which strengthen one's inner self, are to be maintained. For some people, this might bring a huge change in their lifestyle, which is very difficult to adjust within a short period.

People who face extremely difficult circumstances reach deep inside and find inner strength that they were unaware they owned. There have been instances of patients who were on their deathbed, but recovered completely from their diseases due to outstanding willpower and tremendous strength of character. These are nothing but instances where the Higher Self has demonstrated its great value.

Dr. Abraham Maslow, is an expert who has described characteristics of 'O*ur essential inner nature*', which is synonymous to definition of Higher Self. He has discussed how its initially fragile character could be repressed, but not lost entirely.

Maslow says that one cannot love others until he or she learns to love their own self. He came up with some self-actualization *metavalues* like wholeness, perfection, completion, justice, aliveness, richness, simplicity, beauty, goodness, uniqueness, effortlessness, playfulness, truth, and self-sufficiency.

19. How to Imagine and Create an Internal Model of Happiness in Your Mind

There is an old saying, which says that, '*a man becomes what he believes he can.*' Similarly, the world around every one of us is the same. The difference lies in our perception. Little do we realize that this perception is what makes all the difference in shaping up of our entire lives.

Consider how unhappy some people are despite having all the materialistic pleasures and how happy some people are in spite of having nothing. There are examples of famous people who have been miserable or even committed suicide despite having great amounts of money, love, fame, friends, attention, and success in their fields.

No one else can give you happiness. Happiness comes from inside.

You can be given material possessions and someone can give you unconditional love, which is wonderful, but to find happiness you need to set goals, and reach goals. You need to find a basic contentment inside yourself and know that you are worthy of giving and receiving love.

At the end of the day, the truth remains that in this fast life, we tend to lose ourselves in the external world and tend to forget the entire world that lies inside us. The world that focuses on the purity of your soul is always being overshadowed by the external world.

If we try to analyze the situation, it will be seen that we never experience the external world directly. Our focus on the external thoughts. It does not consist of the external world events themselves, but our views associated with those events.

Throughout our life, our mind is always filled with various thoughts. It is almost impossible that our mind goes completely blank and becomes devoid of all the thoughts. Thoughts directly establish our emotions. Our positive emotions like love, joy, and happiness and negative emotions such as anxiety, anger, and depression play an instrumental role in deciding how we react to our external conditions and hence shape up our external world.

Right from the day we are born, we are being exposed to various emotions and thoughts. The lifelong experiences and the kind of environment that we are subjected to determine the person that we become. However, after a certain extent it is entirely our perceptional choice while building our image of our environment.

If we decide to create a world full of beauty, harmony, love, truth, and happiness in our mind, then we will actually start to live in that world! Similarly, if our perception of the world consists of ugliness, conflict, hate, falsehood, and unhappiness, then that will hold true for us. In short, your world will be built based on your own imagination and hence one must learn to think positive and create a world of happiness, which will be pleasurable for everyone.

20. Two Worldviews - Negative versus Positive Thinking

So how do you see your glass? Is it half-full or half-empty? Two descriptions of the same event can be so different in nature! The age-old debate of positive thinking versus negative thinking continues even today. It might be just a matter of perception, but in fact, this little difference can change your life. The ultimate choice you make changes you forever. So, what do you choose to become, an optimist or a pessimist?

Recently, Dr. Roger Sperry, a Nobel-prize winning psycho-biologist wrote about how science is taking this new level of consciousness as a powerful force shaping the present as well as the future of living beings. Connection of psychology and biology is very ancient and holds ground even today.

Groups, societies, and the entire human race can cooperatively develop states of higher consciousness. Reaching that critical mass level can open new doors to opportunities, which were previously beyond our imagination.

Thousands of years ago, humans could live together peacefully only in small groups however, with time our abilities to organize and live together peacefully have evolved. The size of groups that are able to function in harmony has grown from families to tribes, to nations, and eventually to a new world order, that ultimately includes all nations and all people on the face of this earth.

It is a known fact that, powerful creative forces are built into every cell of every living creature. These growth forces are providing the momentum to make this better world a better place to live.

If you have a pessimistic view of the future, you will be inclined to have negative thoughts and depression. However, if you have an optimistic view of the future, you will feel happy and look forward to live and enjoy every single day of your life. If you want to get rid of the roots of your negativism or depression, you must examine and replace negative thoughts with positive reasoning and understanding.

21. How Can You Be Happy in an Imperfect World?

It is very simple to believe and becomes imperative to think of only good things and that life is paradise. However, this is not true. There is nothing like paradise on earth. There are many imperfections, irregularities, negativities, fears, and disillusions. Your ability to cope with these negativities and bounce back emitting positive vibes shows your capability to be happy in an imperfect world.

Life is nothing short of a permanent struggle. You have to abide by the rules of nature. You have to accept both positive and negative sides of existence. Death is as much a reality as life itself. Happiness and unhappiness, pain and relief, predictable and whimsical go hand in hand. If one exists, the other also exists. You cannot dispute those facts.

All these facts stem from your perceptions. You cultivate and inoculate right from wrong, good from evil, and so on. Therefore, you create a picture of an ideal world and then view and compare your circumstances from your world. You try to change everything to suit your preferences.

How to be happy amid such imperfections

The only way to combat this perception is to accept things as they are. What you receive from life and nature is the ultimate. Think, perceive, experience, and accept the world as it is. Do not look at it from behind colored glasses. Once you understand this fact, you can find happiness everywhere and anywhere in this imperfect world.

However, human nature has both optimism and pessimism within. You as an individual can conquer pessimism with your optimism. You err, as you are human. However, if you learn from your mistakes, you evolve into a better individual. You are able to give more to this world. You can spread positive feelings around you and others.

Some of you try to avoid the darker facts of life by allaying their existence. Although it does give you a short reprieve, you fear it in some corner of your heart. Hence, instead of avoiding or dispelling your fears, tackle them by accepting these grim realities of life as coexistent with your basic existence itself. This puts you on a sublime situation and you can locate happiness in facing reality.

22. Deficit Motivation vs. Abundance Motivation

Deficit motivation, as the name suggests, is your belief that whatever you have received or are receiving is much lower than you should receive. Deficit motivation indicates yourself being in scarcity and hence, would appreciate any increases.

This creates a feeling of depression and you seem to harbor ill feelings against others as they have more than you do. You try to take away from others what you feel should rightfully belong to you. Sometimes, you go into a cocoon due to your grievance and apathy.

Abundance motivation indicates loads of everything. You feel that you have much more than your expectations. You dispel extreme satisfaction over your bounty. You possess a feeling of extreme gratefulness.

Whatever you receive beyond is a bonus and you do not harbor any ill feelings. It is a feeling of contentment. Anything else you receive is for your desire and it is not anything that you feel accrues to you. You are happy with what you have and try to share it with others.

However, the glitch here is that your feeling of abundance and deficit does not match with your actual bearings. It is your individual perception. If you set very high goals for yourself, you remain in a state of deficit motivation constantly. You think that you should deserve it. This triggers a set of emotions, which harbor negative feelings like anger, resentment, depression, jealousy, and others.

Rather, if you view whatever you have in terms of abundance motivation, you feel overwhelmed. You feel grateful and experience a deep sense of satisfaction, peace, and happiness. You are able to appreciate the subtleness in everything. You find abundance in nature, your feelings, belongings, and in everyone. Therefore, it leads to assertive or positive thinking and aiming for similar goals. Hence, abundance motivation leads you to further positiveness and optimism in life.

Abundance motivation denotes the powerful motivation from within while deficit motivation points towards victimization. You feel that you lack in everything, as you do not receive it from others. Modifying this concept can help you think that you could give much more to others. This is lodging you on abundance motivation.

Stop and appreciate what you have. Stop and look at what you have achieved in life. If you are reading this, you have achieved learning how to read. Each step as you go on in life, will bring you to small goals and large goals. But, take a moment to relax and appreciate where you have been.

23. How to Develop Positive Thinking and Feel Happier in Everyday Life

You are the sole deciding authority to chart the course of your happiness. You have to decide on how to develop positive vibes within you to make you increasingly happier. Work and develop your feelings towards attainment of happiness. Your measure of happiness is your ultimate concern. Hence, an analysis of your happiness in your everyday life can help you sort out a way to gauge your daily happiness. This instigates a way to maintain continuing happiness in your life.

Although there is both positive and negative all around, you need to put in positive feelings and vibes in negative situations. Your brain is but human and hence, gives rise to all types of feelings and thoughts. Tackle your brain and locate positiveness within negativity.

Every living being has both positiveness and negativity within. Pushing negativity to oblivion and accommodating positiveness within is the essence of life and existence. This creates a harmonious situation in every stage of life. The hardest of criminals has a positive corner within his heart, which needs proper guidance to evolve and crush evil thoughts.

Whenever you face an unpleasant situation, your first reaction is of abhorrence. Nevertheless, do not allow this feeling to grow. Instead, look for something positive amongst or rather within a bad situation. This lightens the situation and makes you progress towards something positive.

It is common to say that evil thoughts stem and roam in an idle brain. Hence, canalize your thoughts positively in your idle or laid-back moments. A constant and regular positive vibe spreads positiveness within you and in others around you.

Analyze the sequence of feelings within you and identify if you have more of positive or negative thoughts in a situation. At the same time, list out the thoughts associated with positive or negative emotions. Normally, your higher self-values like truth, kindness, simplicity, and similar others constitute positive thoughts. Negative feelings stem forth from emotions like failure, fear, rejection, and similar others.

Confront this situation by surrounding yourself with persistent positive thoughts and look for sources to weed out negative feelings. This sure makes you a happier and a much more positive being.

24. Increasing Your Self-Worth to Get Greater Happiness

High self-esteem helps to enhance mental health, life success and happiness. A person who loves himself, his work and his home usually feels happy. A man should have self-respect. There are two kinds of self-esteem one is conditional and other one is unconditional. Conditional self-esteem means that person's self-esteem exists on certain factors like property, wealth, intelligence, etc. and vice versa.

A person should respect himself if he does not, then he will live with an inferiority complex throughout his/her life. He should respect and love himself and others without any conditions. If a person adores himself without a condition then he would be happy to know anything about himself. This love provides him power to overcome fears to face the various challenges in life. In case he does not, he will always criticize himself sometimes for no reasons. This results in his severe depression.

Self esteem is a very important part of happiness.

The level of self-esteem brings confidence. Positive and negative thinking, pains and pleasure teach us good as well as bad things to us. We must learn to save ourselves from negative elements. This is nothing but love for self. Conditional self-love is confidence and unconditional one is self-esteem. Responsibilities bring control, if a person is responsible for his own emotions he has control over his emotions and in turn he will be happy. You must care about your own needs and wants. It includes your work, your skin, your body parts, your home, your accessories, etc. It increases your self-esteem and self-worth. Your main concern should be your own happiness. This does not mean to be selfish. Giving brings happiness, too. But, if you give too much and you are not taking care of yourself, you can put yourself in danger.

Life is give and take in moderation.

Every person has both positive and negative aspects of his life, body, behavior, etc. You should also be aware of your negative elements so, that you can improve them gradually and transform them into your strengths.

Therefore, plan your time and possessions for taking care of your self and your interests to enhance happiness in your life.

25. How to Develop a Positive Self-Image

Self-image is an image of ourselves we have set in our illusion. It is a deposit of sensatory sketches, viewpoint, and opinion regarding ourselves. Perfect self-image is an aspiration of what you want to look like. Self–image is of two kinds – one is ideal self-image and the other one is perceived self-image. Perceived self-image is the real image of us.

Guilt generates from the space between the two types of self-images. Guilt of our images lowers our self-esteem. To overcome guilt we should reduce the gap between Perfect self-image and perceived image. We can either do this to change our perfect image or improve our perceived image. One more way to save ourselves is to create a false image as our perfect image. Accepting or liking ourselves is the first step towards developing the self-esteem. We accept ourselves means accepting other's opinion towards us. During learning try to know the duties of your hated portion of your appearance and you will get to know how important it really is.

Adopt measures to keep your body and mind healthy like exercise, yoga, and get adequate sleep. Increase your confidence through enlarging your self-belief instead of saying this particular quality does not suit you, your age, personality, etc. This kind of flexibility helps us to go at any area of life. This kind of attitude helps us to face any kind of challenge. Negative thinking develops anxiety and nervousness that stops us from proceeding in any direction. Beware of negative emotions such as guilt, depression, and anger. They are the main obstacles in the path of success that lowers our motivation and confidence.

Another way to develop self-esteem is to ignore negative reactions toward us.

Practice positive thinking about yourself; use the right words to describe yourself. Rigidity in this attitude can hurt us with the changes in society, whereas flexibility molds the person according to the external environment.

So, develop a good self-image and be happy.

26. Learn to Accept Self and Others

In Maslow's hierarchy of needs theory, self-actualization is the ultimate goal one wants to achieve. A self-actualized person has no problem in accepting himself and others complete with their positive and negative traits. No human being is perfect and has certain shortcomings. People have difficulty in recognizing their imperfections. Therefore, the first step in solving the problem is to accept the fact that one has certain shortcomings.

Maslow introduced the concept of the higher self in a self-actualized person. This higher self is our prime motivation and drives us towards success and in the search for the unattainable.

Several times parents or friends use derogatory terms to address children when they are unable to perform basic tasks or do badly at school. Children are very sensitive and they perceive these labels negatively as a failure of their intelligence or personality. These children grow into adults with an inferiority complex, carrying a burden of their childhood. In fact, the higher self changes in to one's parents and becomes a part of our lives. We end up trying to meet the expectations of these internalized parents, throughout our lives.

The key to accept one's self and others is by recognizing one's true higher self. One has to learn to acknowledge and love oneself, along with one's negative traits, instead of wishing them away and living in self-denial. One must have a positive outlook in life and remember that we are responsible for ourselves and cannot blame others for our actions or defects. One can achieve self-acceptance by gaining control over one's life, forgetting the past, planning for a bright future and forgiving others for their actions and harsh words.

The self-acceptance process begins with first being truthful to oneself. Next, one has to assess one's strengths and weaknesses and try to overcome them by focusing on the positives. A detailed self-analysis can help one understand the basic reason for falling short of one's expectations. Then one must tap one's higher self to resolve the needs and expectations gap.

This powerful motivator can greatly accelerate the self-acceptance process. In this way, one can take a stepwise approach to accepting oneself and others along with their defects, by having a positive outlook towards life.

27. How to Be More Self-Confident

To be more self-confident, it is important to understand the meaning of self-confidence. Self-confidence is nothing but the chance that a person can do something. Self-confidence stems from a person's belief in himself and his abilities.

Self-confidence develops self-esteem and helps people achieve their goals. Negative thoughts reduce a person's self-confidence and he may not achieve his goals despite the fact that he has the necessary skills and resources for the same. It is necessary to have self-confidence to progress in life. However, one must remember that self-confidence varies with the circumstances and the job on hand. A person can develop his self-confidence by setting goals for his life. Every goal achieved boosts his self–confidence. Similarly, every failure is an opportunity to learn from mistakes and to do better in the future.

One can develop self-confidence only if one believes in oneself. Self-belief gives an individual the power to accomplish his goals. For a person lacking in self-confidence there are several ways to increase self-confidence. The first step is to have a positive self-image. This makes a person strong against the comments and negative criticism from others and he can take on the world. Next, one must analyze our social skills, cognitive skills and self-management skills as they hold the key to our success at work, and in our relationships with others. This analysis tells us where we stand and points out areas for improvement.

We can develop certain skills and learn from others to achieve success and joy in life. Nobody is born equipped with skills; therefore, one can acquire new skills by learning from others and by improving their knowledge of those skills.

Another way to develop self-confidence is by setting realistic goals and then striving to achieve them. Achievement of these goals increases self-confidence. A positive frame of mind and positive reinforcement help one to neutralize negative thoughts and develop self-confidence. A practical approach for raising self-confidence is to practice visual achievement of one's goals. This helps one to focus on the task and think of ways to accomplish the goal. The task is broken into manageable bits and one can plan steps to achieve them.

Therefore, one must have self-confidence since it holds the key to success in their personal and professional life. When you doubt your own abilities, take time to reflect on the things you have learned in life. You'll be amazed at everything you have learned. So, have confidence that you can continue learning everyday. Keep yourself occupied with learning something new everyday. A busy mind makes for a happy mind.

28. Using External vs. Internal Expectations to Evaluate Yourself

Several factors like control and independence govern an individual's personality, relationships, and determine how successful he is in life. There are people who are very dependent on others' approval for their actions. This dependence leads to low self-esteem, depression and failure in relationships, in an attempt to meet others' expectations. These people give more importance to others than to their own power of reasoning. If one feels burdened by the need to do good for others, or has to take their permission before doing any task then these are clear signs that one is in the web of external expectations. One has to learn to break this habit and put themselves before others, without being selfish.

Many times people start depending on others to fulfill their emotional or financial needs by acting weak and helpless. Others think they are indispensable and that the home or workplace cannot run in their absence.

Such people are forever doing things for others and putting themselves under severe stress in the process. This happens when one has low self-confidence and belief in one's capabilities. The solution to this problem lies in taking control of the situation and thinking about oneself without harming the interest of others. An individual's higher self has the ability to know what is best for the person and hence, one must listen to one's inner voice in any situation. This means that it is all right to seek advice and approval from others, but the individual himself must be the decision maker.

The key to internal control lies in first accepting oneself with one's weaknesses. The next step is to believe in oneself and one's capacity to make sound decisions based on one's experience and judgment.

By taking control of one's life one minimizes the need for others in one's life. This is not to say that one must be a lone ranger, but that one must be independent in thought and action. This helps one to take control over one's life and to lead a happy and fulfilled life, without carrying the burden of other's expectations. Hence, the responsibility of tapping into one's internal control lies with the individual himself.

29. Sources of Dependency and External Control

Among individuals, some are every independent and others who are very dependent on others for their basic needs, as well as their personal and financial needs. In the normal scheme of things, a person can fend for himself when left to his resources. However, parents are extremely protective of their children and are on hand to fulfill their every need.

This dependence becomes conditional when children grow up. They can lead independent lives but stay with their parents since they cannot afford the same standard of living as provided by their parents. This situation continues until an individual believes that he/she can be independent. An independent individual is more responsible and competent and is internally strong.

Since man is a social animal, the sources of dependency are limited to family, peer group and reference groups. Society imposes many beliefs and values in individuals. Instead of accepting them at face value, one must analyze everything and then accept it.

People have strong rooted value systems that they inherit from their parents. These values constantly reprimand them throughout life. One must break free of these beliefs by accepting those that are rational and discarding those that are irrelevant; without feeling guilty for doing so. The conflict emerges when our value systems clash with what we actually want to do. An individual who depends on others will feel pressurized and kill his feelings to please others. On the other hand, a person with strong internal control will please himself first and then think of others. In fact, the key to happiness lies in deciding one's interest without harming others.

Surprisingly compliments can be sources of external control. Individuals receive conditional compliments in the promise of undertaking certain tasks. A smart internally controlled person can recognize this manipulation and give no commitment to do the job, while an externally dependent person will go to any extent to fulfill his duties. Therefore, an individual must recognize the sources of dependency and take the steps to overcome them.

30. Sources of Internal Control

Society conditions us to give preference to others over self. This leads to self-deprivation and sacrifice of one's needs and desires for the sake of others. A person who puts self before others is not selfish as long as it doesn't hurt anyone. An individual who is happy and satisfied can make others happy. This is unlike an externally controlled person who is frustrated and burdened by the need to meet others' expectations. Since internal control emanates from within oneself, one has to become more aware of one's needs, ambitions and desires. Recognizing these signals and paying attention to them is the first step to achieving more internal control.

Another way to develop internal control is to look within and to be more conscious of one's feelings. Again, an individual can face a conflict between satisfying self and ignoring the needs of others. The resolution lies in listening to one's higher self. This inner voice knows what is best for the individual and can help resolve such moral issues. An individual with a strong inner self will never compromise his own interest, neither will he offend others. This is a delicate balance, but one can develop one's judgment with experience of several issues.

However, a person has control only over his actions and emotions. He can regulate these activities to satisfy his needs and attain happiness in the process. To develop internal control one must continuously seek external approval and sanction. An individual exercises no power over other people's thoughts and actions. If it is available it is good, else it is beyond one's range of command.

One can strengthen internal control by positive reinforcement and motivation. Having knowledge about things is also helpful in raising internal control. A good way to minimize external control is to have a hobby that keeps one busy and focused. Those who have no interests are more concerned about what others say and continuously seek their opinions. Hence, one must look inward and seek inspiration from one's higher self to strengthen one's internal control.

31. How to Be Internally Directed and Effective with Others

One can focus better on developing internal control if one analyzes the reasons for dependence on external control factors. This analysis gives an insight into one's weaknesses and directions to overcoming those weaknesses. People depend on others in an attempt to avoid responsibility or shift blame. They may seek approval or act in a helpless manner so that others make the decisions. Individuals who are not assertive are internally weak and this leads them to seek external control. Internal weakness stems from a low self-esteem and a lack of self-confidence. A negative outlook towards life acts as a negative reinforcement, and one develops an inferiority complex. Such individuals feel it is selfish to be happy without making others happy. They have a massive fear of loneliness and rejection. Sometimes, they may put on a facade to hide some negative aspect of their personalities.

The first step to break this negative cycle is to accept oneself and to be truthful to oneself. One must learn to put self before others in a way that both parties are happy. One has to face facts and take responsibility for oneself and one's actions. This helps one to be independent and gives immense mental strength to live on one's terms. If a person still lacks confidence, he has to motivate himself about the rewards of internal control and the restrictions of external control. A person controlled by external factors is a weakling and loses all self-respect and independence.

A better way to strengthen one's internal control system is to do some introspection to get in touch with one's inner self. One must remember that social acceptance stems from self-acceptance. Hence, one must love oneself before loving others. One must break away from abnormal relationships and start fresh. It can be painful at first, but one develops a healthy and positive attitude to life without the burdens of a dead relationship. One must trust oneself without entrusting one's future in the hands of others. Ultimately, it is important to remember that the key to internal focus and control lies in a total break from external controlling factors.

32. How to Control Other People

One can develop a strong internal control system by listening to one's higher self. However, there are times when there is a conflict of interest between one's internal control and the external control system. The problem's resolution lies in doing what is best for self without hurting others.

This is a tough decision and one can turn to one's higher self to help in these circumstances. The higher self plays an important role in an internally controlled person. However, one can control others in a number of ways without being rude. The first step is to acknowledge that one is submissive and automatically does things to please others. These feelings create stress and the person is torn between self-interest and satisfying others' expectations. One must then assert oneself and gently refuse to oblige the external forces without feeling guilty.

One can control other people by taking steps to increase one's internal control. This is possible by associating with positive people with healthy lifestyles. One must think independently by keeping away from the external source of control for a while. There is great strength in the power of imagination. One must visualize oneself to be assertive in different situations. This gives the person courage to face the world and to make independent decisions. One must seek a balance between external and internal sources of control so that all parties involved are satisfied and happy.

One must be more observant and not fall for subtle manipulation by external forces from our reference group. One must resolve differences of opinion by listening to the other person and keeping all lines of communication open. It helps to keep a cool head and to focus on the cause of disagreement rather than arguing abusively. One may not listen to the other person, but one must have total respect for his feelings and thoughts.

Therefore, an intelligent individual is one who is assertive without being rude and the path to controlling others thus lies in developing a strong internal control system.

33. How to Achieve Peak Functioning of Your Mind and Body

In this busy world where mind and body are never at peace, it is very important to find a way which can help in the - *peak functioning of Mind and Body.*

Aristotle gave this insight around *2,000* years ago. Since then the importance of relationships between excellent performance and happiness was understood.

While doing a task, if you feel that your mind and body are involved in it, it is the state which helps you perform the best. It makes you feel as if every cell of yours is involved in ones work. It helps you physically as well as mentally.

However, if the condition is opposite, you might have the feelings of prolonged anxiety, anger and depression.

The harmonious experiences, which help you attain peace with optimum outcome on your side, are something which is referred to as "*peak experiences*", in the language of *Maslow*. Here a person feels more integrated and confident.

Harmonious functioning model can help you understand the root causes of motivation and emotion. It provides you with several strategies that can help you gain - peak learning, peak performance and peak happiness.

Harmonious functioning helps the mind and body to function actively. It assists our system, especially - *the cognitive systems* and *conscious processes.*

Too much of challenge, confusion and anxiety cause us to perform low. You do not know what to decide and feel puzzled. On the other hand, if the challenges are less, it brings boredom and depression.

The strongest motivator however, is growth. This growth can be attained through- *knowledge*. Our brain strives for better and organized knowledge. Above all, if you are happy, everything is achieved.

We all want our lives to be free from the tensions and worries that come to us now and then. Our internal force can help us overcome the negative feelings. *Harmonious functioning* helps us attain that peace of mind rewarding us with the motivating force.

34. Optimal Learning as the Basis of Happiness

To attain happiness, it is very important to understand what can help you gain that. Several psychologists came up with their concepts and theories, all focusing on growth as a primary motive.

Let us see how they have presented their views and beliefs -

1. First, let us have a look on the theory of Dr. George Kelly- OPTIMAL LEARNING AS THE BASIS OF HAPPINESS.

Dr. George Kelly wrote a book on *The Psychology of Personal Constructs* in *1955.* He described our basic nature as trying to know the world around us and attempting to adapt to it in the best way.

Dr. Kelly said that we could form several models of a particular thing. It is our brain, which finally chooses the best out of them. He believed that if our beliefs fail to cope with inputs--especially the strong beliefs, we get anxious.

2. Dr. Donald Berlyne with his theory - OPTIMAL STIMULATION AS A BASIC HUMAN MOTIVE.

According to the psychologists, we become unhappy when our biological sub-system either gets over stimulated or under stimulated. The moderate degree is the state of pleasant feelings.

Dr. Berlyne said that our brains seek to maintain an optimum level of stimulation. He believed that the desire for knowledge is the most powerful motivational force.

3. Third comes Dr. Mihaly Csikszentmihalyi with his theory of OPTIMAL CHALLENGE CAUSES THE FLOW EXPERIENCE.

Dr. Mihaly Csikszentmihalyi wrote the book *The Psychology of Optimal Experience.* He believed that happiness could be achieved through the control of the Flow of mind.

His theory had similarity with the theory of *Dr. Kelly's*. Both focused on optimum levels of matching between inputs and cognitive abilities.

4. Last but not the least, comes Dr. Stephen Grossberg with his theory of ADAPTIVE RESONANCE IN NEURAL NETWORKS UNDERLIES LEARNING, MOTIVATION, AND AROUSAL.

According to him, when we learn something significant, some neural network [cognitive subsystem] resonates.

An optimal degree of matching between input and expectations causes resonance.

35. How Does Harmonious Functioning Affect Happiness

A harmonious functioning of your body and inner self produces positive outcomes. The immediate outcomes of such functioning are excellent performance, understanding, learning an activity, and immense happiness and satisfaction. Although these form the immediate outcomes, there are many other associated results.

These associated results could evolve later. Some of them are an increased liking for a particular work, better physical health, and a boost to your self-confidence. You feel the joy of being able to do something excellently and bring happiness and harmony to self and others.

If you develop an increased liking for any activity, you experience a feeling of peace and tranquility while performing the activity. This feeling of peace and tranquility elevates your level of happiness. This elevation comes from the harmonious functioning of your physical self and your mental self. Coordinated functioning stimulates you and increases motivation levels.

Anything you enjoy, you do not mind repeating your performances. Rather, your performances at every repeat display higher proficiency levels. You enjoy, receive motivation, perform, and feel happy and satisfied at your performance. Such performances can be anything ranging from watching a movie, solving puzzles, reading a book, dancing to a tune, or anything else. The activity is only a zone to highlight your efficiency.

Such harmonious functioning helps you identify your likings and disliking. You rather try to analyze and identify the reasons for your love or dislike for an activity. If you dislike dancing to a tune, you do not enjoy it and consequently, you do not experience any happiness from dancing.

Sometimes developing a harmonious liking to something you have disliked previously can kindle your love for it. You dislike an activity as you lack the motivation to perform in it. This could also be the same the other way round. You do not perform well in an activity as you lack the motivation for it. Hence, kindling motivation could make you view the activity in a different light. You then create an interest in it. Slowly, you develop a harmony in it and perform better. This leads to increased happiness and satisfaction.

36. How Does Harmonious Functioning Affect Emotions

People who lead balanced lives have control over their emotions.

Harmonious functioning refers to a comfort region within which an individual is happy. In case something upsets this balance, he experiences discomfort and tries to restore the balance. Individuals who have learned to control and regulate this balance lead happy, harmonious lives.

The brain exercises control over our emotion. It has mechanisms to tackle all types of extreme situations so that the balance is not disturbed. When we are happy, there is positive energy and the brain is very alert and hyperactive. Thus, the brain responds well to positive stimuli. If we are unhappy, negative emotions take over and produce annoyance, concern and monotony. An individual achieves accord when the brain receives just enough stimuli that it can handle and develop well enough.

The underlying system that governs emotions is satisfaction of our values. Our values include needs for recognition, financial independence and love from family and friends. One experiences tension, and worries about satisfying these values when one cannot fulfill them. One can control emotions better when one can understand the underlying values.

All individuals comprise of many parts that make up the whole. All these divisions have different aspirations. One is happy when one can meet these wishes. Unhappiness results when any of these wishes are not satisfied. A person has varying emotions depending on the circumstances at the time. One feels joy or sadness during times of change. These emotions are pointers to the fact that something is not right. It implies a disturbance in the values that we hold dear. People can view these changes as a chance for greater learning and personal enhancement.

One can perform better in life when one recognizes what are one's values and how they contribute to a harmonious functioning. One must make a list of one's values in all aspects of life, such as work and relationships. Then one must examine if they are meeting their expectations and values. If not, one must take the steps to fulfill them. Doing so restores one's harmonious balance and a person comes back into his comfort zone. Hence, the key to a harmonious function lies in understanding our emotions and learning to control them.

37. How Mental Control Increases Your Level of Happiness

A person is happy if he wants to be happy. An unhappy individual can never be content. He will always hold somebody else responsible for his misery. The onus for happiness lies with oneself and not with any external forces. The earlier we realize this; the easier the road to contentment. External forces are beyond our control while we can master our own thoughts and actions that lead to happiness.

We can focus inward which makes it easier to accept the external forces. We cannot change external forces, but we can face them and tackle their effect as they play some role in our lives. If an individual has problems in his personal relationships or at the workplace, it may seem like the end of the road and people slip into severe depression. They key to happiness lies in recognizing the problem and then taking positive steps to solve it. This gives a semblance of control and one feels confident to take on the world.

One can break the cycle of external control by modifying one's thoughts. The first thought is that external conditions are not necessary for personal happiness. We have total control over our feelings. With these sets of values one can exercise mental control and ignore the fears of external control.

Inward control gives us the strength to be positive and optimistic. We develop a positive attitude to life and this enhances our personality. We must break the dependence on external factors and take control of our lives.

If there are too many problems in life and they seem insurmountable, one must practice dissociation. One must not take it as a sign of weakness, but think with a clear head and from the perspective of an outsider. This can give us some direction towards resolving the problems.

One has to take charge for one's actions and for one's happiness, by connecting with our inner higher self. This is possible by first examining what is lacking in life and then developing an action plan to overcome that situation. Thus, one observes that practicing mental control gives one strength and control over one's life and leads to contentment and happiness.

38. Learn to Be a Master of Your Emotions

Most people are subject to both positive and negative emotions.

They get depressed over the state of their lives, work and finances. Similarly, they are overjoyed when prospects brighten in the same spheres of life. However, this can create havoc in one's life. An individual needs to exercise control over his emotions so that he can have a stable life.

One can master emotions in a number of ways. The first is to get rid of the feeling of helplessness.

One must spend time in pursuing activities that one likes.

One must try to convert all negative energy and thoughts into positive ones. This is possible if one thinks of enjoyable ways of doing the same mundane activities.

One must first assess the nature of activities that one is performing. Then one must convert a majority of these tasks into those that one enjoys and discard those tasks that seem boring or a punishment. This will make a person happy for the maximum period since he will be in his region of comfort while performing the enjoyable tasks.

It is not always possible to avoid all boring activities. Therefore, one must think of alternatives, which give better ways of doing the same job. One cannot wish away unpleasant thoughts and actions, but it is possible to control certain parameters that enhance our lives. By adopting this approach, one can make time for activities that are more enjoyable. This helps one to develop a positive attitude to life and improves the quality of life.

Sometimes it is just not possible to make time for pleasure. However, one can still cope with bad situations by changing one's mental makeup. One can think positively and create an action plan to get out of the bad situation. Overcoming bad experiences in life gives one the courage to tackle life's problems positively and to take responsibility for one's lives.

One must view things positively since this restores harmony and brings positive emotions to the fore. Having a positive outlook in life is therefore the best way to control one's emotions.

39. Resolve Your Inner Conflicts to Bring Harmony and Happiness

A person comprises of many parts, based on the roles he plays in life. He is an employee, a husband, a father and a husband, all at the same time. He has to fulfill different expectations of these roles simultaneously. This leads to a conflict and he ends up dissatisfied and unhappy. This is because the conflict disturbs his comfort zone and impairs his harmonious functioning.

The best way to resolve inner conflicts is to first realize the problem, examine it and then think of options to overcome it. This basic understanding of the problems resolves the burden of conflict. One must develop a positive frame of mind to tackle inner conflicts. One must try to develop unity between inner motivations and external activities. Every action has positive and negative consequences. Expectation of positive outcomes helps one overlook the negativity associated with a particular activity.

Positive expectation has a harmonious effect on the mind and the body and this gives one the energy to carry out the task.

Many times, we have reservations or problems about particular tasks. The best way to overcome this is to analyze the root cause for these reservations. We must go beyond the symptoms to the real reason for the problems. Once we identify this, we can work better and our efficiency increases, else these problems keep nagging us and weighing us down.

Once we overcome these internal conflicts, we can experience a balance and return to the comfort region of our lives. Every problem has a solution if we keep in mind that our goal in life is to be happy and that we undertake all activities to attain joy and harmony in life. Another potential area of conflict is what we must do versus what we really want to do. Again, we must do that which makes us happy without hurting others.

Therefore, the path to resolving inner conflicts lies in achieving a balance between what brings happiness to oneself and others. Also, between short-term and long-term goals. We can achieve harmony and happiness if we use positive reinforcement to motivate ourselves.

40. Looking at a Problem from a Higher Level of Understanding

All individuals have fears and problems. These problems may be regarding work, family, finances or an illness. It is easier to get anxious and weighed down by them. We have to cope with these problems and move on in life. First, one must examine the underlying reasons for a problem to understand it. Then one must design a plan of action to overcome it.

Life is full of important incidents and events. One cannot predict all of them, but one can prepare to face them. In times of emergency, this preparedness helps the individual to overcome the problem or handle it effectively. Hence having a roadmap for success is important. One can learn from the experience of others in similar situations, to solve problems. This gives us confidence because people have successfully applied the method to good effect.

Next, one must look at every problem as an event, analyze the causes for it and then think of the possible outcomes. If one wants to learn new skills or a sport, one can emulate experts mentally, or read self-help books to learn the same. Since the required result is to master the skill, one takes great effort in the learning process to be successful. Some aspects of the learning process are beyond our control, but we can visualize the internal processes of the experts that led to achievement of desired results.

We must assess the best methods to achieve the best results and then practice continuously to achieve perfection. Usually our brain does an analysis of every event by itself. When the brain does not do this, one must conduct an analysis to find the best way to achieve the desired result.

Finally approaching a problem from a higher perspective gives us objectivity to find the required solution. One must try to look at the higher issues in a problem because the brain feels pressurized to seek the reasons for this threat to one's higher beliefs. This higher self gives us a better understanding of problems and acts as a cushion in the face of adversity. It strengthens our inner control systems and helps resolve problems that we face periodically in life.

41. How to Overcome Depression and other Negative Emotions

We put great pressure on ourselves by setting high goals for achievement, whether in our personal or professional lives. Inability to meet these expectations causes stress and results in depression. We develop low self-esteem and start doubting our abilities. This leads us to sink in to a negative cycle with a very bleak future. This is a wrong approach to life and needs to be changed. We must not punish ourselves for not meeting unrealistic expectations. It is better to lower our limits and then devote all energies to fulfilling those goals. Those who set low standards, are capable of much more and must raise their goals higher.

Another reason for depression is the pressure of our reference group. This comprises friends, family and co-workers. People feel a responsibility to meet their aspirations and go to unreasonable lengths to achieve the same. It is better to change the frame of reference and compare one's performance with the relevant group since this increases our confidence when we can achieve the set goals.

It is important to remember that we cannot control external factors, but internal control is possible over our own thoughts and actions. We must take steps to restore our inner harmony so that we are always in the comfort zone of our lives. Hence, one must modify our thoughts and actions to achieve the set ideals in life. This gives us motivation and a confidence to tackle the task. When situations change, one should modify the goals and the motivating factors along with these changing circumstances.

One must choose ideals that are stimulating in case one is under motivated to make the tasks more interesting. One must change one's perspective and view the advantages or positive outcomes of any event or activity. This ensures that one enjoys the work and is happy. Therefore, the best way to overcome depression and other negative emotions is to set practical and realistic goals in life to ensure satisfaction and a sense of achievement in the individual.

42. How to Overcome Grief, Sadness and Apathy in Your Life

People battle a number of negative emotions like grief, apathy and sadness in life, resulting from underachievement or a lack of meaning in life. This leads to low self-esteem and a negative outlook towards life in general.

The main reason for this state of mind is a lack of objectives in life. If one leads an empty meaningless life, there is no motivation for any actions and the person vegetates. This lacuna can be due to factors beyond one's control; in which case one can do little to change the situation. So incase this lack of objectives is due to internal factors like failure, one must set better and new objectives to lead a better meaningful life.

Other reasons for grief and apathy are mainly a purposeless life, low ability or very high aims that are impossible to achieve. Some people may be bad at time management and hence feel overwhelmed by the tasks, while some are dependent on others to fulfill all their personal, emotional and financial needs.

However, it is possible to tackle all negative feelings and individuals can emerge stronger from such experiences. Those who lack self-confidence can read self-help books and learn techniques to be more assertive. Those who believe in avoidance must learn to live for themselves. They must put themselves before others, without feeling guilty. They must set achievable goals and reasonable expectations for themselves. When a task is broken down into smaller parts, it seems attainable. One can solve all problems in life by examining the reasons for their occurrence. This gives strength and confidence to face the challenges of life.

Usually grief, apathy and sadness stems from under stimulation of our senses. Hence, we must set higher standards for ourselves and concentrate on the results to motivate ourselves. We can break down each task into smaller sub tasks so that the job becomes interesting. Next, one can seek competition from peers to make the job interesting. To relieve monotony, one can view the job from a different perspective that can give it a new dimension and meaning. Therefore, the means to overcome grief, apathy and sadness in life lies with the individual himself.

43. How to Lower Your Anxiety and Stress and Increase Confidence

Every generation has different problems, but they are facing these problems under one sign and that is Anxiety and Stress. They are not very big words, but they can do some big damage. These two can cause emotional breakdown and disappointment.

To get rid of anxiety and stress you must lower your goals and anticipation level. When you set your goal low, then it will be easy for you to accomplish your mission. This will decrease your chances of failing.

To avoid negative feelings that disturb your mind, make multiple goals and practice hard to give attention to every area such as career, relationships, family, being alone, health, finances, and recreation. Our mind continues to hallucinate the memories of the past until it makes similar understanding with new ones in life.

With multiple goals, you need to focus on each goal simultaneously. You must classify your goals according to your priorities as process goals and outcome goals. **Process goals** are those that we do in response to outside world and **outcome goals** are those, which brings changes in outside world because of our efforts. Anxiety develops, when we try to fulfill those goals that are out of our control.

To be successful and happy you must prefer growth-oriented and energetic aims. Stationary goals will be complete at a certain point in time but dynamic goals need continuous actions. Dynamic goals improve your capabilities and efforts, human body and gray matter are dynamic in nature that makes its adjustable with the changes in surroundings. Dynamic goals bring success, growth and happiness in life.

Slow and steady wins the race. Follow systematic desensitization. Take one-step at one point of time. Divide your time in accordance with your small goals to acquire that big aim of your life.

Psychologists recommend these guidelines to remove anxiety and depression of failure from your life. Make life happy as well as ambitious by following the above guidelines.

44. Learn to Be Happy in All Situations

In situations like an interview or waiting for results one can get anxiety. The state of uncertainty causes angst or anxiety. To remain happy in all situations, we should always think not only positive about the outcome, but what positive action you can take if what you hope for doesn't work out.

Optimism controls our emotions mentally. It very much depends on confidence. The source of optimistic thoughts is confidence in ourselves and in forces in the outside world. Optimism increases with the increased control over results. An external cause for good outcome is nature, luck, fortune, etc.

It is waste of time to find an excuse for our failure. You simply cannot blame yourself or anyone else. It is better to utilize that extra time to think about the cause of the problem and the remedy of the problem.

Proper control over your thoughts brings a positive attitude towards life. We must learn to be happy and patient in every kind of situation. We need to learn to accept success and defeat graciously. Sometimes when you lose, someone else wins. Hey, rejoice for the other person and try harder next time.

To remain happy and optimistic we must trust the ultimate force that tackles each person in the world like God, nature, and evolution.

We must work according to laws of universe.

Everything that is happening has its cause. Learn from the mistakes and move ahead.

45. How to Funnel Your Energy to Maximize Happiness

The best way to refresh your energy is to focus on your positive points and turn away your attention from the negative points.

Various situations cause anxiety in a person that depress the person and results in his gloom or unhappiness. For an example, the stress of appearing for tests is common among students. Because of this anxiety, some students fail to do well in their exams.

The best way to overcome anxiety is to throw out every negative thought from your mind. Positive thoughts will help you keep your eyes on your goal. If you have a proper control over your mind, you will be able to focus on your subject matter and your performance.

While doing your work, you need to focus. Avoid negative thoughts, pessimism or glumness. Remember, negative thoughts or pessimism stop you from being a winner. In your free time, think about the ways to improve your performance. Victorious people concentrate deeply on their life goals to gain success. When you focus on your goals, you will achieve success and eventually success brings joy for you.

A person is wholly responsible for his unhappiness. Focus in life helps you to overcome positively to bad situations and attain happiness in your life.

Taking steps to learn how to control your emotions will give you more control over life period, which in turn, will bring you more happiness.

To attain success, a person must have full control over his or her psyche and a strong control over his emotions.

46. How to Stay in Control of Your Life and Be Happy

If a person wants to be happy, he must give first precedence to happiness over other things. To be happy one should know his values and his habits. Our behavior is nothing but stimulus-response type of communication with its environment. Habit becomes habit because it meets with our ethics. These habits have programs in our mind that is why it is always present in our life routines.

To be happy we need to use the conscious part of our aptitude. Our brain needs O-PATSM a system to make sure that our habits should match with the values. In an O-PATSM system, one is going to analyze his or her habits weekly, make a list and plan for a whole week about work, objectives, and wants. Then you need to take time from your busy schedule for yourself to engage in nature walks, pleasure reading, aerobic dancing, calling friends, attending social events, etc.

Life should not be all work and no play. And, life should not be all play and no work.

There should be a proper balance between every area of life like travel, home, profession, finances, self-development and relationships.

Some people sacrifice their present need for future benefits. This holds motivation to do better in future. People need to balance his or her present and future rewards. Otherwise a person cannot enjoy his or her life in present time. Looking to the future can make the present miserable and boring.

Make a proper list of your needs according to their importance and create dreams or small goals. Reaching small goals bring momentary wins.

Think about your values, their relevance, importance and ways to fulfill them through limited energy and sources. It is better to change your needs from time to time and learn to enjoy these needs by taking time to reevaluate your goals.

47. How to Achieve Your Goals in Life and Be Happy

Your goals in life are your aims in life. You strive to achieve your goals for personal satisfaction. You plan them in your growing or essentially teenage years. Goals are according to your dreams in life. You aspire to accomplish each of them. Later, you feel immense satisfaction on accomplishment of your goals.

It is essential to achieve your goals in life to be happy and satisfied. Follow certain guidelines for successful accomplishment of your goals:

It is necessary to form goals in life as otherwise you are a rudderless boat. Nevertheless, it is wrong to attach excessive importance to any particular goal. If for any reason, you are unable to accomplish a particular goal, do not lose heart. Instead, look for alternatives and find happiness at accomplishment of the new goal.

Another successful way of attaining happiness through your goals is to have various goals. Essentially blocking all avenues and concentrating on a single goal cannot always provide happiness and satisfaction. Among your choice of goals, you can identify and prioritize them so that you can keep moving forward and not moan over non-accomplishment or inability to satisfy any particular goal.

Giving unto others is an important and useful attribute. It also highlights your concern for others. Your goals can never be in isolation. Hence, giving due consideration to others' happiness and looking after their needs and satisfaction of their goals can also prove to be a means of making you happy.

Developing confidence in your abilities to work and make your dreams come true is an essential prerequisite for gaining happiness through your goals. Besides, your ability to give or help others instead of being at the receiving end boosts your inner self. You realize that you can take care of yourself independently.

Fix steps in your goals or rather break them into smaller and simpler achievement levels. Your final goal is the outcome of these smaller goals on your path to achieve your main goal.

Try to keep your goals at a realistic level with sufficient clarity and keep moving forward.

48. How to Manage Your Time and Create Happiness in Your Life

Life is essentially a juggle between times to accomplish your goals.

A planned juggle provides sufficient time to work for your goals, have time for yourself, and accomplish goals consistently. Rushing through your work often makes you tired and unconnected to your goals. Everything then becomes monotonous.

To maintain sufficient clarity in your goals, manage time efficiently by identifying and prioritizing your goals. Write down a checklist and conduct regular self-evaluation sessions. These help you grade your progress and boost your confidence to work towards your goals better.

It may seem simple to set priorities but accomplishing them accordingly should be your main target. Following guidelines could help you in your path towards attainment of happiness by satisfaction of your goals:

All your goals and activities need prioritization. Categorize important activities as to which of them provide you and others maximum happiness.

Some goals are long-term while some need immediate attention. Try to create a balance between long-term and immediate goals with self versus other's happiness goals. Give equal importance to all.

It is not humanly possible to do everything always. Enjoy your work to increase your productiveness. Otherwise, you miss on the essentiality of the goals, which is being happy.

Try to maintain a systematic way of organizing everything. Haphazard working cannot bring in efficiency and consequently, your aim suffers.

In the same vein, overdoing things is also ineffective in attaining your goals. In your rush to do everything perfectly, you spend more time and energy on any one work disregarding others. Alternatively, you keep working trying out your enthusiasm and fun of working towards your goals.

Put a clear demarcation line between goals for yourself and that of others. You can help others in their progress towards their goals, but forgoing yours for the sake of others is foolishness. A family functions through the cooperative efforts of every member. A single member juggling time to maintain and fend for all members of the family is an irrational situation. Teach your children to help. It teaches them self-assurance and makes them feel needed and part of the family.

You can locate your happiness by taking free time off everything to concentrate on your efforts and progress over past period. This self-analysis gives you an idea of your productiveness.

49. Your Checklist about How to Be Happy

It is essential to be happy to succeed and progress in life. You choose your goals, actions, beliefs, and thoughts forming the key contributors to your happiness. Hence, you can decide and maintain a checklist of your happiness by following certain guidelines:

Your happiness should be the essential goal in your life as you hold the key to your emotions and feelings. Do not hold others or their actions responsible for causing you unhappiness. Choose your path through the obstacles of life to land at a state of happiness for you and others too.

Unconditional love is the essence of happiness. The feeling of loving someone is to accept the person unconditionally without placing any importance on presence or absence of specific characteristics. Such love erodes all negativity and lends a positive direction to your life by giving and attaining happiness for all.

Health, forgiveness, self-acceptance, and empathy form the pillars of unconditional love and consequent happiness. Working towards good health for all is a preexisting element of happiness. Strive to take great care of your health. Loving is forgiving. Accepting others as they are and viewing mistakes or wrongdoings as a part of enlightenment process is a huge leap towards happiness.

Personal growth lends greater value in your quest for happiness. You then assign more priority to various values of higher life like simplicity, goodness, self-sufficiency, aliveness, uniqueness, justice, and similar others.

Never assign extreme priority or attachment to any particular goal or any situation. Extreme attachment causes anxiety and acts in the opposite direction of your goal to be happy.

Develop a sense of balance and respect everyone's view. Form your opinions, but do not overreact to other's views and feelings. As an individual, everyone has the right to believe and decide goals. Your inner sense of balance can help overcome conflicting situations and make you happy in all your activities.

Do not give in to any fears as this negative feeling stands in your way to be happy. Maintain positive feeling and associated aura around you to forever progress ahead in your quest for happiness in any situation.

It is said that those that are the happiest have:

A routine. They go to bed at the same time each night and arise at the same time each morning.

They get adequate exercise.

They are married.

They have a hobby they enjoy.

They know how to set goals in increments and meet those goals.

They have a spiritual belief system.

They get sunlight. (Sunlight is important)

They have a pet.

They are satisfied with their job and feel they are a special part of the universe.

They have learned to control their emotions.

They know how to give, and how to receive graciously.

They find time to relax and to laugh. Laughing is a great outlet and allows you to release stress. So laugh. If you don't have a great sense of humor, find what does make you laugh. Have a great big belly laugh ☺

Then try to find a reason to laugh every day.

www.ingramcontent.com/pod-product-compliance
Lightning Source LLC
Chambersburg PA
CBHW081418080526
44589CB00016B/2590